MITCHELL LEY

DIGITAL TWINS: Crafting Tomorrow's Realities with Today's Data

Table of Contents

INTRODUCTION

Digital twins represent a revolutionary concept in the realm of technology and industry, transforming the way we design, monitor, and manage physical systems. A digital twin is a virtual replica or simulation of a physical entity, system, or process. This digital representation is not just a static model but a dynamic and real-time reflection of its physical counterpart, constantly updated with data from sensors, IoT devices, and other sources. The concept of digital twins has gained significant traction across various industries, including manufacturing, healthcare, infrastructure, and more.

KEY COMPONENTS OF DIGITAL TWINS:

Physical Entity:

The digital twin starts with a physical entity, whether it's a machine, a building, a vehicle, or even an entire city. This physical object serves as the anchor for the digital twin, and the goal is to create a comprehensive and accurate virtual counterpart.

Virtual Representation:

The digital twin is not a mere 3D model; it is a highly detailed and accurate virtual representation of the physical entity. This representation encompasses not only the geometry and structure but also the behavior, functionality, and operational characteristics of the physical object.

Real-time Data Integration:

One of the defining features of digital twins is their ability to continuously receive real-time data from sensors, actuators, and other connected devices associated with the physical entity. This data flow allows the digital twin to mirror the current state of the physical counterpart.

IoT and Connectivity:

The Internet of Things (IoT) plays a crucial role in the implementation of digital twins. Sensors embedded in the physical object gather data on various parameters such as temperature, pressure, motion, and more. This data is then transmitted to the digital twin, ensuring that it stays synchronized with the real-world conditions.

Simulation and Analytics:

Digital twins leverage advanced simulation and analytics capabilities. By running simulations on the digital twin, stakeholders can predict and analyze the performance, maintenance needs, and potential issues of the physical entity. This proactive approach helps in optimizing operations and minimizing downtime.

AI and Machine Learning:

Artificial Intelligence (AI) and Machine Learning (ML) algorithms are often integrated into digital twins to enhance their predictive and analytical capabilities. These technologies enable the digital twin to learn from historical data, identify patterns, and make intelligent predictions about future behavior.

APPLICATIONS OF DIGITAL TWINS:

Manufacturing and Product Design:

Digital twins are used to simulate and optimize the manufacturing process, improving efficiency and reducing defects. In product design, digital twins help engineers visualize and test prototypes before physical production.

Smart Cities and Infrastructure:

In the context of smart cities, digital twins can model and monitor entire urban environments, from transportation systems to energy grids. This aids in urban planning, resource optimization, and emergency response.

Healthcare:

Digital twins in healthcare can replicate the human body or specific organs to simulate medical conditions, enabling personalized treatment plans and surgical simulations. This technology is particularly valuable in precision medicine.

Energy and Utilities:

Digital twins are employed to monitor and optimize energy production and distribution. This includes simulating the behavior of power plants, predicting equipment failures, and ensuring the efficient use of resources.

Aerospace and Defense:

In aerospace, digital twins are utilized to model aircraft components and systems, allowing for predictive maintenance, performance optimization, and virtual testing.

ORIGINS AND EVOLUTION OF DIGITAL TWINS

The concept of digital twins has its roots in various fields, evolving over time as technology advanced and industries sought more sophisticated ways to understand and manage physical entities.

Early Conceptualizations

- The early seeds of digital twins can be traced back to computer-aided design (CAD) and simulation tools in the 1960s and 1970s.
- Engineers and designers began creating virtual models to simulate and test the performance of physical systems before actual production.

NASA's Influence

- NASA played a pivotal role in the development of early digital twin concepts.
- During the Apollo missions, NASA used digital models to simulate spacecraft and predict potential issues before they occurred in the real world.

Emergence in Manufacturing

- The manufacturing industry embraced digital twins in the 1990s as computer-aided design and computer-aided engineering became more sophisticated.

- Manufacturers used virtual prototypes to optimize production processes and reduce the need for physical prototypes.

Integration of IoT and Sensors

- The true evolution of digital twins accelerated with the rise of the Internet of Things (IoT) in the 2000s.

- Integration of sensors into physical entities allowed for real-time data collection and transmission to digital replicas.

Industry 4.0 and Smart Manufacturing

- The Industry 4.0 movement, starting around 2011, emphasized the integration of digital technologies into manufacturing.

- Smart manufacturing systems leveraged digital twins for predictive maintenance, quality optimization, and overall process efficiency.

Expanding Beyond Manufacturing

- Digital twins moved beyond manufacturing into various industries such as healthcare, construction, and energy.
- The concept broadened to encompass not only products but also processes, systems, and entire urban environments.

Advancements in Simulation and Analytics

- Advancements in simulation and analytics technologies further propelled the evolution of digital twins.
- Real-time data analytics, machine learning, and artificial intelligence enhanced the predictive capabilities of digital twins.

Cross-Industry Collaboration

- Cross-industry collaboration became a driving force in the evolution of digital twins.
- Knowledge and best practices from one industry began influencing and enriching the applications in others.

Current State and Future Trends

- As of the latest developments, digital twins are integral to various industries, enabling predictive maintenance, optimizing performance, and supporting decision-making.

- Future trends include the integration of augmented reality (AR), virtual reality (VR), and the development of collaborative digital twin ecosystems.

Challenges and Opportunities

- The evolution of digital twins has not been without challenges, including data security concerns, interoperability issues, and the need for standardization.

- However, these challenges present opportunities for innovation, collaboration, and the establishment of robust frameworks.

Understanding the origins and evolution of digital twins provides a foundation for appreciating the depth of their impact on modern industries. From conceptual beginnings to widespread adoption, digital twins continue to shape how we design, monitor, and optimize the physical world.

KEY CHARACTERISTICS OF DIGITAL TWINS

Digital twins are dynamic, data-driven virtual replicas of physical entities, and they possess several key characteristics that set them apart from traditional static models. These characteristics contribute to their ability to provide real-time insights, facilitate predictive analysis, and optimize the performance of physical systems. Here are the key features:

Real-Time Data Integration

- Definition: Digital twins continuously receive real-time data from sensors, IoT devices, and other sources associated with the physical entity.

- Significance: This characteristic ensures that the digital twin is a live and up-to-date representation, mirroring the current state and conditions of its physical counterpart.

Dynamic and Evolving

- Definition: Unlike static 3D models, digital twins are dynamic, reflecting changes and updates in real-time as the physical entity undergoes alterations or experiences variations.

- Significance: This dynamism allows for a more accurate representation of the current state, enabling better decision-making and performance optimization.

Comprehensive Virtual Representation

- Definition: Digital twins go beyond simple geometry; they incorporate detailed information about the structure, behavior, and functionality of the physical entity.
- Significance: This comprehensive representation enables a deeper understanding of the physical system, fostering more accurate simulations and predictions.

IoT and Sensor Integration

- Definition: Digital twins leverage the Internet of Things (IoT) by integrating sensors and connected devices to gather data on various parameters such as temperature, pressure, and motion.
- Significance: IoT integration enhances the fidelity of the digital twin, allowing for a more granular and real-time understanding of the physical entity's state.

Simulation and Predictive Analysis

- Definition: Digital twins incorporate simulation capabilities to predict future behaviors and outcomes based on historical data and real-time inputs.
- Significance: This feature enables stakeholders to anticipate potential issues, optimize performance, and conduct virtual testing before implementing changes in the physical world.

Artificial Intelligence and Machine Learning

- Definition: Many digital twins integrate artificial intelligence (AI) and machine learning (ML) algorithms to analyze data, identify patterns, and make intelligent predictions.
- Significance: AI and ML enhance the digital twin's ability to learn from experience, adapt to changing conditions, and provide more accurate insights over time.

Lifecycle Representation

- Definition: Digital twins cover the entire lifecycle of a physical entity, from design and manufacturing to operation, maintenance, and eventual decommissioning.

- Significance: This end-to-end representation allows for a holistic view, supporting decision-making at every stage and optimizing the entire lifecycle.

Cross-Domain Applicability

- Definition: Digital twins are applicable across various industries and domains, including manufacturing, healthcare, smart cities, aerospace, and more.
- Significance: This versatility highlights the adaptability of digital twins to different contexts, fostering cross-industry collaboration and knowledge sharing.

Interconnectivity and Collaboration

- Definition: Digital twins can be interconnected to create collaborative ecosystems where multiple digital twins interact and share information.
- Significance: This collaborative feature supports more holistic views of interconnected systems, promoting better coordination and efficiency.

User Interface and Interaction

- Definition: Digital twins often include user interfaces that allow stakeholders to interact with the virtual representation, visualize data, and make informed decisions.

- **Significance**: A user-friendly interface enhances the accessibility of the digital twin, enabling a wider range of users to leverage its insights.

Understanding these key characteristics provides insight into why digital twins are considered transformative tools in various industries, offering unparalleled capabilities for monitoring, analyzing, and optimizing physical systems.

COMPONENTS OF A DIGITAL TWIN

A digital twin is a complex and dynamic virtual representation of a physical entity, comprising various interconnected components. These components work together to create a comprehensive and accurate digital counterpart to its physical counterpart. Here are the key components of a digital twin:

Physical Entity

- Definition: The physical entity is the real-world object, system, or environment that the digital twin represents.
- Significance: The physical entity serves as the anchor for the digital twin, and the accuracy of the digital twin depends on how well it mirrors the characteristics and behavior of the physical counterpart.

Virtual Representation

- Definition: The virtual representation is the digital counterpart of the physical entity, created using computer-aided design (CAD) models or other digital modeling techniques.
- Significance: This digital model goes beyond simple geometry, incorporating detailed information about the

structure, composition, behavior, and functionality of the physical system.

Real-Time Data Integration

- Definition: Real-time data integration involves the continuous flow of data from sensors, IoT devices, and other connected sources associated with the physical entity to the digital twin.

- Significance: Real-time data ensures that the digital twin remains synchronized with the current state of the physical entity, providing accurate and up-to-date information.

IoT Devices and Sensors

- Definition: IoT devices and sensors are embedded in or connected to the physical entity to collect data on various parameters such as temperature, pressure, motion, and more.

- Significance: These devices contribute to the real-time data integration, enhancing the granularity of information and supporting more accurate simulations and predictions.

Communication and Connectivity

- Definition: Communication and connectivity components enable the exchange of data between the physical entity, sensors, and the digital twin.

- Significance: Effective communication infrastructure ensures that data is transmitted seamlessly, allowing for continuous updates and real-time monitoring.

Simulation Models

- Definition: Simulation models within the digital twin enable the replication of the physical entity's behavior and responses to different conditions.

- Significance: Simulation models support predictive analysis, allowing stakeholders to anticipate how the physical entity will react to changes and make informed decisions.

Artificial Intelligence (AI) and Machine Learning (ML) Algorithms

- Definition: AI and ML algorithms analyze data from the physical entity and sensors, identifying patterns, making predictions, and adapting to changing conditions.

- Significance: These algorithms enhance the digital twin's ability to learn from historical data, improving accuracy and providing intelligent insights over time.

User Interface (UI) and Visualization Tools

- Definition: The user interface allows stakeholders to interact with the digital twin, visualize data, and interpret insights.
- Significance: An intuitive and user-friendly interface makes the digital twin accessible to a broader range of users, facilitating better decision-making.

Data Storage and Management

- Definition: Data storage and management components handle the storage, organization, and retrieval of data associated with the digital twin.
- Significance: Effective data management ensures that historical data is retained, supporting analytics, and providing a comprehensive view of the physical entity's lifecycle.

Security and Privacy Measures

- Definition: Security measures, including encryption and access controls, protect the integrity and confidentiality of the data associated with the digital twin.

- Significance: Robust security measures are essential to safeguard sensitive information and ensure the trustworthiness of the digital twin.

Understanding these components helps in appreciating the complexity and functionality of digital twins, which are designed to be holistic and adaptable representations of their physical counterparts, supporting various applications across industries.

REAL-TIME DATA INTEGRATION AND CONNECTIVITY

Real-time data integration and connectivity are foundational elements of digital twins, enabling the continuous flow of information between the physical entity and its virtual counterpart. These components are crucial for maintaining synchronization, providing up-to-date insights, and supporting dynamic decision-making. Let's delve deeper into these key aspects:

Real-time Data Integration

- Definition: Real-time data integration involves the seamless incorporation of data from sensors, IoT devices, and other connected sources into the digital twin in real-time.

Importance:

- Dynamic Reflection: Real-time integration ensures that the digital twin dynamically reflects the current state and conditions of the physical entity.
- Accuracy: It enhances the accuracy of the digital twin by incorporating the latest information, allowing for precise monitoring and analysis.

Internet of Things (IoT) Devices and Sensors

- Definition: IoT devices and sensors embedded in or connected to the physical entity collect data on various parameters.

Importance:

- Granularity: These devices provide granular, real-time information, contributing to a detailed understanding of the physical entity.
- Continuous Monitoring: Real-time data from sensors facilitates continuous monitoring of conditions, performance, and other relevant metrics.

Communication and Connectivity

- Definition: Communication and connectivity components enable the exchange of data between the physical entity, sensors, and the digital twin.

Importance:

- Seamless Flow: Effective communication infrastructure ensures the seamless flow of data, preventing delays or disruptions in information transfer.

- Continuous Updates: Connectivity supports continuous updates, keeping the digital twin synchronized with changes in the physical world.

Edge Computing

- Definition: Edge computing involves processing data closer to the source (at the edge of the network) rather than relying solely on centralized cloud servers.

Importance:

- Reduced Latency: Edge computing reduces data processing latency, allowing for quicker responses and real-time analysis.
- Bandwidth Optimization: It optimizes bandwidth usage by processing critical data locally and transmitting only relevant information.

Data Validation and Quality Assurance

- Definition: Processes for validating and ensuring the quality of incoming data before integration into the digital twin.

Importance:

- Reliability: Ensures that the data integrated into the digital twin is reliable, accurate, and free from errors.
- Decision Confidence: High-quality data enhances confidence in decision-making based on digital twin insights.

Time-Series Databases

- Definition: Time-series databases are optimized for handling data points indexed by time, which is crucial for managing real-time data in digital twins.

Importance:

- Temporal Context: Time-series databases maintain temporal context, supporting historical analysis and trend identification.
- Efficient Retrieval: Facilitates efficient retrieval of time-stamped data, essential for analytics and simulation.

Security Measures

- Definition: Security measures, including encryption and access controls, protect the integrity and confidentiality of real-time data.

Importance:

- Data Protection: Safeguards sensitive information from unauthorized access or tampering, ensuring the trustworthiness of the digital twin.
- Compliance: Addresses security and privacy concerns, aligning with regulatory and industry standards.

Predictive Analytics and Machine Learning

- Definition: Real-time data integration supports predictive analytics and machine learning algorithms that analyze current and historical data for intelligent insights.

Importance:

- Proactive Decision-Making: Enables proactive decision-making by predicting future trends and potential issues.
- Adaptability: Machine learning algorithms adapt to changing conditions, improving the accuracy of predictions over time.

Collaborative Ecosystems

- Definition: Connectivity enables digital twins to exist in collaborative ecosystems where multiple digital twins interact and share information.

Importance:

- Holistic Views: Collaborative ecosystems provide holistic views of interconnected systems, promoting better coordination and efficiency.
- Inter-Digital Twin Communication: Supports communication and information exchange between different digital twins, enhancing overall system intelligence.

Real-time data integration and connectivity form the backbone of digital twins, ensuring that these virtual replicas remain dynamic, accurate, and responsive to changes in the physical world. The seamless flow of information enables organizations to harness the full potential of digital twins for monitoring, analysis, and optimization across various industries.

SIMULATION AND ANALYTICS IN DIGITAL TWINS

Simulation and analytics are integral components of digital twins, empowering stakeholders to gain insights, make informed decisions, and optimize the performance of physical entities. These components go beyond static representation, enabling dynamic modeling, predictive analysis, and real-time feedback. Here's a detailed exploration:

Simulation Models

- Definition: Simulation models within a digital twin replicate the behavior and characteristics of the physical entity in a virtual environment.

Functionality:

- Predictive Capabilities: Simulation allows stakeholders to predict how the physical entity will respond to different conditions and scenarios.
- Virtual Testing: Facilitates virtual testing of changes or improvements before implementation in the physical world.

Predictive Analytics

- Definition: Predictive analytics involves analyzing historical and real-time data to make predictions about future trends, behaviors, or events.

Functionality:

- Anticipating Issues: Predictive analytics identifies potential issues or failures, allowing for proactive maintenance and risk mitigation.
- Optimization: Supports the optimization of processes, resource allocation, and decision-making based on anticipated outcomes.

Artificial Intelligence (AI) and Machine Learning (ML)

- Definition: AI and ML algorithms analyze data from the digital twin to identify patterns, make predictions, and adapt to changing conditions.

Functionality:

- Learning from Data: Machine learning algorithms learn from historical and real-time data, improving their accuracy over time.

- Pattern Recognition: AI and ML enhance the digital twin's ability to recognize complex patterns and correlations within data.

Dynamic Behavioral Modeling

- Definition: Dynamic behavioral modeling involves capturing and representing the changing behaviors of the physical entity over time.

Functionality:

- Adaptable Representations: Dynamic models adapt to changes in the physical entity's behavior, ensuring an accurate representation in the digital twin.
- Continuous Evolution: The digital twin evolves dynamically as the physical entity undergoes changes or variations.

Scenario Analysis

- Definition: Scenario analysis involves simulating different scenarios to understand potential outcomes and their implications.

Functionality:

- Risk Assessment: Helps assess risks and uncertainties by modeling various scenarios and their likelihood.
- Decision Support: Provides decision-makers with insights into the potential consequences of different courses of action.

Performance Optimization

- Definition: Performance optimization involves using simulation and analytics to enhance the efficiency and effectiveness of the physical entity.

Functionality:

- Efficiency Gains: Identifies areas for improvement and suggests changes to optimize performance and resource utilization.
- Continuous Monitoring: Supports continuous monitoring and adjustment of processes for ongoing optimization.

Failure Prediction and Proactive Maintenance

- Definition: Analytics in digital twins can predict potential failures based on patterns and anomalies in data.

Functionality:

- Reduced Downtime: Enables proactive maintenance by predicting when components are likely to fail, reducing downtime.
- Cost Savings: Minimizes unplanned maintenance costs by addressing issues before they escalate.

Data Visualization and Interpretation

- Definition: User interfaces in digital twins present data in a visually accessible manner, aiding interpretation and decision-making.

Functionality:

- User-Friendly Interface: Visualization tools make complex data comprehensible to users, facilitating effective communication.
- Interactive Dashboards: Users can interact with dashboards to explore data, trends, and insights in real time.

Continuous Improvement Feedback Loops

- Definition: Feedback loops involve using insights from analytics and simulations to refine and improve the digital twin over time.

Functionality:

- Iterative Development: Supports an iterative approach to digital twin development, incorporating lessons learned and adjusting models for continuous improvement.
- Adaptive Systems: Enables the digital twin to adapt and evolve based on feedback and changing conditions.

Cross-Domain Integration

- Definition: Integration of simulation and analytics across various domains allows for a holistic understanding of interconnected systems.

Functionality:

- Interconnected Insights: Enables stakeholders to consider the impact of changes or events in one domain on others.
- Comprehensive Decision-Making: Supports comprehensive decision-making by considering multiple factors and their interdependencies.

Simulation and analytics in digital twins provide a dynamic and intelligent foundation for understanding, managing, and optimizing complex physical systems across diverse industries. The ability to simulate, analyze, and learn from data fosters a proactive and data-driven approach to decision-making and system management.

AI AND MACHINE LEARNING INTEGRATION

The integration of artificial intelligence (AI) and machine learning (ML) plays a crucial role in enhancing the capabilities of digital twins. These technologies empower digital twins to analyze complex data, identify patterns, make predictions, and adapt to changing conditions. Here's a detailed exploration of AI and ML integration in digital twins:

Data Analysis and Pattern Recognition

Functionality:

- Complex Data Handling: AI and ML algorithms handle large volumes of complex data generated by sensors and other sources.

- Pattern Identification: These technologies excel at identifying intricate patterns and correlations within the data.

Predictive Analytics

Functionality:

- Predicting Future Trends: AI and ML enable digital twins to predict future trends and behaviors based on historical and real-time data.
- Proactive Decision-Making: Predictive analytics supports proactive decision-making by anticipating outcomes and potential issues.

Anomaly Detection

Functionality:

- Identifying Abnormalities: AI and ML algorithms excel at detecting anomalies or deviations from expected behavior.
- Early Issue Detection: Anomaly detection contributes to the early identification of issues or irregularities in the physical entity.

Adaptive Learning

Functionality:

- Learning from Data: Machine learning algorithms continuously learn from historical and real-time data, improving their understanding of the physical entity.
- Adapting to Changes: Adaptive learning allows digital twins to adapt to changes in the behavior or conditions of the physical system.

Optimization Algorithms

Functionality:

- Efficiency Improvement: AI and ML-powered optimization algorithms suggest changes to enhance the efficiency of processes and resource utilization.
- Continuous Monitoring: These algorithms continuously monitor performance and recommend adjustments for ongoing optimization.

Failure Prediction and Proactive Maintenance

Functionality:

- Predicting Failures: AI and ML models predict potential failures by analyzing data patterns associated with historical failures.

- Proactive Maintenance: These predictions enable proactive maintenance, reducing downtime and minimizing unplanned outages.

Natural Language Processing (NLP) and Communication

Functionality:

- Human-Machine Interaction: NLP facilitates communication between users and the digital twin through natural language interfaces.

- Data Interpretation: NLP helps in interpreting textual data, enhancing the comprehensibility of insights.

Context-Aware Decision Support

Functionality:

- Contextual Understanding: AI and ML enable digital twins to understand the context of data and events, providing more nuanced decision support.
- Adaptive Responses: The digital twin can adapt its responses based on the specific context of the physical entity.

Cognitive Computing

Functionality:

- Reasoning and Problem Solving: Cognitive computing capabilities allow digital twins to engage in reasoning and problem-solving tasks.
- Intelligent Responses: These capabilities contribute to more intelligent and contextually aware responses.

Continuous Improvement Feedback Loops

Functionality:

- Iterative Learning: AI and ML integration support continuous learning and improvement, allowing the digital twin to adapt to evolving conditions.
- Feedback-Driven Development: Insights gained from analytics and AI-driven processes inform iterative development and refinement.

Personalization and Customization

Functionality:

- Tailored Recommendations: AI and ML enable the digital twin to provide personalized recommendations based on the unique characteristics and requirements of the physical entity.
- Customized Solutions: These technologies support the customization of solutions to specific needs and conditions.

Collaborative Learning in Ecosystems

Functionality:

- Inter-Digital Twin Communication: AI facilitates communication and information exchange between different digital twins within collaborative ecosystems.
- Shared Knowledge: Collaborative learning enhances the collective knowledge and insights of interconnected digital twins.

The integration of AI and machine learning brings a layer of intelligence to digital twins, enabling them to evolve, adapt, and provide increasingly sophisticated insights. These technologies contribute to the transformative potential of digital twins across various industries by making them more adaptive, predictive, and responsive to the complexities of the physical world.

APPLICATIONS ACROSS INDUSTRIES

Digital twins have transformative applications across diverse industries, leveraging their ability to replicate, monitor, and optimize physical entities. Here are applications across various sectors:

Manufacturing and Industry

- Design and Prototyping: Digital twins aid in virtual design and prototyping, allowing manufacturers to optimize products before physical production.
- Smart Factories: Implementation of digital twins in Industry 4.0 for real-time monitoring, predictive maintenance, and production optimization.

Healthcare

- Patient-Specific Treatment: Digital twins of patients enable personalized treatment plans, considering individual variations and responses.
- Medical Imaging Simulation: Simulating medical imaging procedures to enhance diagnostic accuracy and optimize treatment strategies.

Aerospace and Defense

- Virtual Testing: Simulating aircraft performance and behavior to enhance design, optimize fuel efficiency, and ensure safety.

- Maintenance Optimization: Predictive maintenance using digital twins to minimize downtime and extend the lifespan of aerospace assets.

Smart Cities

- Urban Planning: Digital twins model entire city infrastructures for efficient urban planning and resource allocation.

- Traffic Management: Real-time simulation for optimizing traffic flow, predicting congestion, and enhancing transportation systems.

Energy and Utilities

- Predictive Maintenance for Infrastructure: Digital twins monitor the health of energy infrastructure, predicting maintenance needs and preventing failures.

- Optimizing Energy Consumption: Real-time monitoring and analysis to optimize energy consumption in smart grids and buildings.

Automotive

- Vehicle Design and Testing: Digital twins support virtual design and testing of vehicles, optimizing performance and safety.
- Predictive Maintenance: Anticipating and preventing mechanical issues through real-time monitoring and analysis.

Retail

- Supply Chain Optimization: Digital twins optimize supply chain processes, enhancing inventory management and demand forecasting.
- Customer Experience Enhancement: Creating digital twins of retail spaces to analyze customer behavior and optimize layout and product placement.

Construction and Infrastructure

- Building Information Modeling (BIM): Digital twins aid in BIM for efficient design, construction planning, and infrastructure management.
- Predictive Construction: Simulating construction processes to optimize schedules, resource allocation, and identify potential issues.

Telecommunications

- Network Optimization: Digital twins model telecommunications networks, optimizing performance, identifying bottlenecks, and predicting outages.
- Predictive Maintenance: Anticipating equipment failures and optimizing maintenance schedules for telecommunications infrastructure.

Environmental Monitoring

- Ecosystem Simulation: Digital twins simulate environmental conditions, aiding in the study of ecosystems and the impact of changes.

- Climate Modeling: Simulating climate patterns and predicting environmental changes for informed decision-making.

Maritime and Offshore Industry

- Asset Monitoring: Digital twins monitor the condition of maritime assets, predicting maintenance needs and ensuring safety.
- Operational Optimization: Real-time simulation for optimizing ship routes, fuel consumption, and overall operational efficiency.

Education and Training

- Training Simulations: Digital twins support training simulations for various industries, allowing personnel to gain practical experience in a virtual environment.
- Educational Models: Creating digital twins of educational spaces to optimize layouts and resources for enhanced learning experiences.

Entertainment and Gaming

- Virtual Worlds: Creating digital twins of virtual environments for immersive gaming experiences.

- Character Simulation: Simulating characters with AI-driven behaviors, enhancing realism in gaming and entertainment.

Finance and Banking

- Fraud Detection: Digital twins model customer transactions to detect anomalies and potential fraudulent activities.
- Risk Management: Simulating market conditions and economic scenarios for risk assessment and decision support.

These applications demonstrate the versatility of digital twins, showcasing their potential to revolutionize processes, improve efficiency, and drive innovation across a wide range of industries. The ongoing advancements in technology and the increasing integration of AI and IoT continue to expand the possibilities and impact of digital twin applications.

CHALLENGES AND CONSIDERATIONS

While digital twins offer tremendous benefits, their adoption comes with several challenges and considerations. Addressing these issues is crucial to maximizing the effectiveness of digital twins in various industries:

Data Security and Privacy

- Challenge: The vast amounts of sensitive data collected by digital twins raise concerns about data security and privacy.

- Consideration: Implement robust cybersecurity measures, encryption, and access controls to protect digital twin data. Adhere to privacy regulations and best practices.

Interoperability

- Challenge: Integrating digital twins with existing systems and ensuring interoperability across different platforms and technologies can be complex.

- Consideration: Standardization efforts and open communication protocols can help overcome interoperability challenges. Choose solutions that adhere to industry standards.

Complexity of Implementation

- Challenge: Implementing digital twins can be complex, requiring expertise in data analytics, simulation, and domain-specific knowledge.
- Consideration: Engage with experienced professionals and consider phased implementations. Start with smaller-scale projects to build expertise and gradually scale up.

Cost of Implementation

- Challenge: The initial costs of developing and implementing digital twins, including sensors, IoT devices, and analytics infrastructure, can be substantial.
- Consideration: Conduct a cost-benefit analysis, focusing on long-term gains in efficiency, predictive maintenance, and operational optimization.

Data Quality and Accuracy

- Challenge: Digital twins heavily depend on the quality and accuracy of the data fed into them. Inaccurate or unreliable data can lead to flawed simulations and predictions.

- Consideration: Establish data quality standards, conduct regular data audits, and invest in sensor calibration and maintenance.

Scalability

- Challenge: Scaling digital twin implementations to cover larger and more complex systems can be challenging.
- Consideration: Design digital twin architectures with scalability in mind. Choose solutions that can handle increased data volume and complexity as the system expands.

Regulatory Compliance

- Challenge: Compliance with industry regulations and standards may pose challenges, especially in sectors with stringent data protection and safety regulations.
- Consideration: Stay informed about regulatory requirements, ensure data handling practices comply with standards, and involve legal experts in the implementation process.

Ethical Considerations

- Challenge: The use of digital twins raises ethical questions, especially when dealing with personal data or potentially influencing real-world decisions.
- Consideration: Establish ethical guidelines for data usage, transparency, and decision-making. Involve stakeholders in ethical discussions and decision-making processes.

Skill Gaps

- Challenge: There may be a shortage of skilled professionals with expertise in data science, AI, IoT, and domain-specific knowledge.
- Consideration: Invest in training programs for existing staff, collaborate with educational institutions, and consider partnerships with specialized service providers.

Change Management

- Challenge: Implementing digital twins often involves significant changes in workflows and processes, which may face resistance from employees.
- Consideration: Implement effective change management strategies, involving employees in the process, providing

training, and communicating the benefits of digital twin adoption.

Long-Term Maintenance and Updates

- Challenge: Ensuring the continued effectiveness of digital twins over the long term requires regular maintenance, updates, and adaptation to technological advancements.
- Consideration: Develop a maintenance plan, stay informed about technological developments, and allocate resources for ongoing updates and improvements.

Cultural Shift

- Challenge: Adopting digital twins may require a cultural shift within an organization, embracing data-driven decision-making and a more collaborative approach.
- Consideration: Foster a culture of innovation and continuous improvement. Communicate the benefits of digital twins and involve employees in the adoption process.

Navigating these challenges and considerations requires a strategic approach, collaboration across different functions, and a commitment to ongoing improvement. By addressing these issues, organizations can unlock the full potential of digital twins and realize the benefits they bring to efficiency, decision-making, and innovation.

FUTURE TRENDS AND INNOVATIONS

As technology continues to advance, several trends and innovations are expected to shape the future of digital twins, expanding their capabilities and applications across various industries. Here are some key trends to watch for:

Integration of 5G Technology

- Description: The deployment of 5G networks will enhance data transmission speeds and reduce latency, facilitating real-time communication and data exchange for digital twins.

- Impact: Faster and more reliable connectivity will enable more complex and dynamic digital twin applications, especially in areas like smart cities, healthcare, and manufacturing.

Edge Computing for Real-Time Processing

- Description: Edge computing involves processing data closer to the source, reducing the need for centralized cloud processing. This will be particularly beneficial for real-time analysis in digital twins.

- Impact: Lower latency, improved responsiveness, and more efficient data processing will enhance the performance of digital twins, especially in scenarios where real-time decision-making is critical.

Extended Reality (XR) Integration

- Description: Digital twins combined with augmented reality (AR) and virtual reality (VR) technologies will enable immersive experiences for training, maintenance, and collaboration.

- Impact: XR integration will enhance the visualization and interaction with digital twins, offering more intuitive ways for users to engage with complex data and simulations.

Advancements in Artificial Intelligence (AI)

- Description: Continued advancements in AI, including deep learning and reinforcement learning, will enhance the analytical capabilities of digital twins.

- Impact: AI-driven digital twins will become more adept at learning from data, making predictions, and adapting to changing conditions, leading to more intelligent and autonomous systems.

Blockchain for Data Security

- Description: Blockchain technology will be leveraged to enhance the security and integrity of data in digital twins, ensuring traceability and preventing unauthorized tampering.

- Impact: Increased data security and transparency will foster trust in digital twin systems, particularly in industries where data integrity is crucial, such as healthcare and finance.

Digital Twins in the Internet of Things (IoT) Ecosystems

- Description: Digital twins will play a central role in large-scale IoT ecosystems, where interconnected devices and systems collaborate and share data.

- Impact: The integration of digital twins with IoT will enable more comprehensive and interconnected views of complex systems, leading to improved decision-making and efficiency.

Generative Design for Innovation

- Description: Generative design, powered by AI algorithms, will be employed in the early stages of product development to explore and optimize design possibilities.

- Impact: Digital twins incorporating generative design will accelerate innovation by quickly identifying optimal design solutions, especially in manufacturing and engineering.

Digital Twins for Sustainable Development

- Description: Digital twins will be utilized to model and optimize sustainability practices in urban planning, infrastructure development, and resource management.

- Impact: Enhancing the role of digital twins in sustainable development will contribute to more eco-friendly and resource-efficient solutions across various industries.

Digital Twins for Personalized Medicine

- Description: Digital twins of individual patients, incorporating genetic, lifestyle, and medical data, will be used for personalized treatment planning.

- Impact: Personalized digital twins in healthcare will lead to more effective and tailored medical interventions, optimizing patient outcomes.

Autonomous Digital Twins

- Description: Digital twins equipped with autonomous decision-making capabilities will be deployed in scenarios where real-time responses are essential.
- Impact: Autonomous digital twins will enable systems to adapt and respond dynamically to changing conditions without constant human intervention, enhancing efficiency and responsiveness.

Digital Twins in Space Exploration

- Description: Digital twins will be utilized to simulate and monitor spacecraft, rovers, and habitats in space exploration missions.
- Impact: Digital twins will play a crucial role in mission planning, equipment monitoring, and troubleshooting in the challenging environment of space.

Human-Digital Twin Interaction

- Description: Advances in natural language processing and human-computer interaction will enable more seamless communication and interaction with digital twins.

- Impact: Improved human-digital twin interfaces will make these technologies more accessible and user-friendly, expanding their adoption across various user groups.

Cyber-Physical Digital Twins

- Description: The convergence of digital twins with cyber-physical systems will create more holistic representations of the physical world with embedded computational intelligence.

- Impact: Cyber-physical digital twins will enable tighter integration between the virtual and physical realms, providing a more accurate and dynamic representation of complex systems.

The ongoing evolution of digital twins will likely see a convergence of technologies, enabling more sophisticated, interconnected, and intelligent applications across industries. These trends reflect the continual pursuit of leveraging digital twins to enhance efficiency, decision-making, and innovation in a rapidly evolving technological landscape.

IMPLEMENTATION STRATEGIES

The successful implementation of digital twins involves careful planning, collaboration, and the integration of various technologies and processes. Here are key strategies to consider when implementing digital twins:

Define Clear Objectives

- Clearly define the goals and objectives of implementing digital twins. Identify specific challenges or opportunities you aim to address, such as improving efficiency, reducing downtime, or enhancing decision-making.

Holistic System Mapping

- Map the entire system, process, or asset that the digital twin will represent. Understand the interconnected components, data flows, and dependencies to ensure a comprehensive and accurate representation.

Select Appropriate Technology Stack

- Choose a technology stack that aligns with your organization's needs and capabilities. Consider the integration of IoT devices, cloud computing, AI, and other relevant technologies based on your requirements.

Data Governance and Quality Assurance

- Implement strong data governance practices to ensure data quality, integrity, and security. Establish protocols for data validation, cleansing, and ongoing maintenance to uphold the accuracy of the digital twin.

Collaborative Cross-Functional Teams

- Form cross-functional teams that include experts from domains such as IT, data science, engineering, and operations. Foster collaboration and communication among team members to ensure a holistic approach to implementation.

Iterative Development Approach

- Adopt an iterative development approach to build and refine the digital twin gradually. Start with a minimum viable product (MVP) and incorporate feedback from users and stakeholders to enhance the system over time.

User Training and Change Management

- Provide comprehensive training to users who will interact with the digital twin. Implement change management strategies to address resistance, and ensure that users are comfortable with the new processes and technologies.

Interoperability Considerations

- Design digital twins with interoperability in mind. Ensure compatibility with existing systems, and if possible, use open standards and protocols to facilitate integration with other platforms.

Security Measures

- Implement robust security measures to protect sensitive data associated with the digital twin. Employ encryption, access controls, and secure communication protocols to safeguard against cyber threats.

Real-Time Data Integration

- Prioritize real-time data integration to keep the digital twin synchronized with the physical entity. Implement efficient mechanisms for data transmission and processing to support dynamic, up-to-date simulations.

COLLABORATIVE DIGITAL TWINS

Collaborative digital twins represent a paradigm shift in the way digital twin technology is applied, emphasizing interconnectedness and collective intelligence. In a collaborative digital twin environment, multiple digital twins interact, share information, and collectively contribute to a more comprehensive understanding of complex systems. Here's an exploration of collaborative digital twins:

Definition

- Collaborative digital twins involve the integration and interaction of multiple digital twins within a shared ecosystem. These digital twins can represent interconnected entities, systems, or processes, and they collaborate to achieve common goals.

Interconnected Systems

- Collaborative digital twins often model interconnected systems where the behavior of one entity can impact or influence others. This interconnectedness allows for a more holistic representation of the entire ecosystem.

Key Characteristics

- Inter-Digital Twin Communication: Digital twins within a collaborative environment can communicate with each other, exchanging information and insights.

- Shared Data and Insights: Information and insights from one digital twin can be shared with others, creating a collective knowledge base.

- Real-Time Collaboration: Collaboration occurs in real-time, enabling dynamic responses to changes or events in the physical environment.

Applications Across Industries

- Manufacturing Ecosystems: Collaborative digital twins in manufacturing can represent various interconnected processes, from supply chain logistics to production lines, fostering improved coordination and efficiency.

- Smart Cities: In urban planning, collaborative digital twins can model various city elements, such as transportation systems, energy grids, and public services, to optimize overall city functionality.

- Healthcare Networks: Collaborative digital twins in healthcare can represent patient care pathways, medical facilities, and associated processes, enabling coordinated and personalized healthcare delivery.

Benefits

- Holistic Insights: Collaborative digital twins provide a more comprehensive view of interconnected systems, allowing stakeholders to understand the impact of changes across various components.

- Improved Decision-Making: By sharing insights and information, stakeholders can make more informed decisions that consider the broader context of the entire ecosystem.

- Efficiency Gains: Coordination and collaboration between digital twins can lead to efficiency gains, optimizing processes and resource utilization.

Technologies Driving Collaboration

- IoT Integration: The integration of Internet of Things (IoT) devices in collaborative digital twins facilitates real-time data exchange and enhances the accuracy of representations.

- Advanced Analytics: Advanced analytics, including machine learning and predictive modeling, contribute to the collective intelligence of collaborative digital twins by identifying patterns and trends.

Challenges and Considerations

- Data Security: Collaborative digital twins involve the sharing of sensitive information, necessitating robust data security measures to protect against unauthorized access or tampering.

- Interoperability: Ensuring seamless communication between different digital twins requires addressing interoperability challenges, especially when using diverse technologies.

Future Trends

- Decentralized and Blockchain Integration: The integration of blockchain technology can enhance the security and transparency of collaborative digital twins, supporting decentralized data sharing.

- Edge Computing: Edge computing can facilitate faster and more efficient collaboration by processing data closer to the source, reducing latency.

Use Cases

- Supply Chain Collaboration: Collaborative digital twins in supply chain management can model and optimize the flow of goods and information across various stakeholders.

- Ecosystem Resilience Planning: In environmental and ecological contexts, collaborative digital twins can simulate and plan for ecosystem resilience by considering the interconnectedness of species, habitats, and climate factors.

Collaborative digital twins represent a powerful approach to understanding and managing complex systems in an interconnected world. As technology continues to evolve, the collaborative aspect of digital twins is likely to play a crucial role in addressing the challenges of increasingly interconnected and dynamic environments.

HUMAN-MACHINE INTERACTION IN DIGITAL TWINS

Human-Machine Interaction (HMI) in digital twins involves the ways in which humans interact with and influence the behavior of digital twins, as well as how digital twins provide valuable information to enhance human decision-making. This interaction is crucial for leveraging the full potential of digital twin technology across various industries. Here's an exploration of key aspects of human-machine interaction in the context of digital twins:

User Interfaces

- Visualization Tools: Digital twins often use advanced visualization tools to represent complex data in a comprehensible manner. User interfaces (UIs) can include 3D models, dashboards, and interactive displays.

- Augmented Reality (AR) and Virtual Reality (VR): AR and VR technologies are increasingly integrated into digital twin interfaces, offering immersive experiences for users to interact with and explore digital representations of physical entities.

Natural Language Processing (NLP)

- Communication: NLP facilitates natural language communication between users and digital twins. Users can interact with the digital twin using spoken or written language, making it more accessible to individuals without specialized technical knowledge.

- Voice Commands: Voice-activated commands allow users to query, instruct, or receive information from the digital twin, enhancing the user experience.

Remote Monitoring and Control

- Real-Time Monitoring: HMI enables users to monitor the real-time status and behavior of physical entities represented by digital twins, allowing for timely decision-making.

- Remote Control: In some cases, users can remotely control or adjust parameters of physical systems through the digital twin interface, optimizing operations.

Decision Support Systems

- Data Interpretation: Digital twin interfaces provide tools for interpreting complex data. Visualization and analytics tools help users understand trends, anomalies, and insights derived from the digital twin.

- Scenario Analysis: Users can simulate and analyze different scenarios within the digital twin environment, supporting decision-making by assessing the potential outcomes of various actions.

Training and Simulation

- Training Environments: Digital twins serve as training environments, allowing users to simulate and practice procedures in a virtual setting. This is particularly valuable in industries such as healthcare, aerospace, and manufacturing.

- Operational Readiness: Digital twins contribute to operational readiness by enabling personnel to familiarize themselves with systems and processes before they are deployed in the real world.

Context-Aware Decision Support

- Contextual Understanding: Digital twins, with advanced AI capabilities, can understand the context of user queries and provide more nuanced and context-aware responses.

- Adaptive Responses: The digital twin can adapt its recommendations and insights based on the specific context of the physical entity it represents.

Collaboration and Knowledge Sharing

- Multi-User Environments: Some digital twins support collaboration by allowing multiple users to interact with the system simultaneously, fostering teamwork and knowledge sharing.
- Shared Insights: Users can share insights, annotations, and notes within the digital twin environment, creating a collaborative space for decision-making.

Feedback Loops and Learning

- Continuous Improvement: User interactions with digital twins can contribute to feedback loops, informing developers and system administrators about areas for improvement and optimization.
- Adaptive Systems: Digital twins can adapt and evolve based on user feedback, creating more user-friendly and effective systems over time.

Mobile and Cross-Platform Accessibility

- Mobile Applications: Many digital twins offer mobile applications, allowing users to access information and interact with the system on-the-go.

- Cross-Platform Integration: Seamless integration with various platforms ensures that users can access and interact with digital twins using their preferred devices.

Ethics and Responsible AI

- Transparency: HMI in digital twins should prioritize transparency, helping users understand how the system works, how decisions are made, and the ethical considerations involved.

- User Empowerment: Users should have control over the digital twin, and ethical considerations should prioritize user empowerment, privacy, and informed consent.

Personalization and Customization

- Tailored Experiences: Digital twins can provide personalized experiences, tailoring information and insights based on individual user preferences and roles.

- Customized Dashboards: Users may have the ability to customize dashboards and interfaces to suit their specific needs and priorities.

Human-Machine Interaction is a critical element in realizing the full potential of digital twins. As technologies continue to advance, the focus on user experience, intuitive interfaces, and ethical considerations will be pivotal in shaping how humans interact with and derive value from digital twins across diverse industries.

ETHICAL CONSIDERATIONS

The deployment of digital twins raises various ethical considerations that organizations and stakeholders must carefully navigate. Ensuring responsible and ethical use of this technology is crucial for building trust, safeguarding privacy, and minimizing potential negative impacts. Here are key ethical considerations in the implementation of digital twins:

Data Privacy

- Challenge: Digital twins often involve the collection and processing of vast amounts of data, some of which may be sensitive or personally identifiable.

- Consideration: Implement robust data privacy measures, including encryption, anonymization, and strict access controls. Adhere to relevant data protection regulations and obtain informed consent when necessary.

Security Concerns

- Challenge: The interconnected nature of digital twins and the reliance on data exchange introduce security vulnerabilities that may be exploited by malicious actors.

- Consideration: Prioritize cybersecurity measures, including encryption, secure communication protocols, regular security audits, and employee training on security best practices.

Algorithmic Bias and Fairness

- Challenge: The algorithms used in digital twins may inadvertently perpetuate biases present in historical data, leading to unfair or discriminatory outcomes.

- Consideration: Regularly audit and assess algorithms for biases. Implement measures to address bias, promote fairness, and ensure that decisions made by digital twins do not disproportionately impact certain groups.

Informed Consent

- Challenge: Users and stakeholders may not fully understand the implications of participating in or interacting with digital twins.

- Consideration: Prioritize transparency and provide clear information about how data will be used. Obtain informed consent from individuals whose data is being utilized, especially in scenarios involving personal or sensitive information.

Ownership of Data

- Challenge: Determining ownership and control of data within a digital twin ecosystem can be complex, especially in collaborative or interconnected environments.

- Consideration: Clearly define data ownership and control mechanisms. Establish agreements and policies that address data ownership, usage rights, and responsibilities among relevant stakeholders.

Transparency and Explainability

- Challenge: The decision-making processes of digital twins, especially those driven by artificial intelligence, may lack transparency, making it challenging for users to understand how decisions are reached.

- Consideration: Prioritize transparency and provide explanations for the decisions made by digital twins. Make efforts to ensure that users can understand and interpret the insights and recommendations generated by the system.

Environmental Impact

- Challenge: The computational resources required for large-scale digital twin implementations can contribute to environmental impact, particularly if not managed efficiently.

- Consideration: Implement energy-efficient computing practices, explore sustainable data center options, and consider the environmental implications when scaling digital twin systems.

Accessibility and Inclusivity

- Challenge: In some cases, digital twin interfaces may not be accessible to all users, leading to potential exclusion of certain groups.

- Consideration: Design digital twin interfaces with accessibility in mind. Ensure that interfaces are usable by individuals with disabilities and consider diverse user needs to promote inclusivity.

Unintended Consequences

- Challenge: The complexity of digital twin systems may lead to unintended consequences or outcomes that were not anticipated during the design and implementation phases.

- Consideration: Regularly assess and monitor the impact of digital twin systems. Be prepared to address and mitigate unintended consequences through ongoing evaluation and adjustments.

Responsible AI Development

- Challenge: Ethical considerations are particularly relevant when implementing AI-driven digital twins, as the decisions made by these systems can have significant real-world consequences.

- Consideration: Adhere to ethical AI principles, conduct ethical impact assessments, and involve ethicists or external experts in the development and deployment of AI-driven digital twins.

Social and Economic Impacts

- Challenge: The deployment of digital twins may have social and economic implications, including job displacement or changes in societal dynamics.

- Consideration: Consider the broader societal impact of digital twins and implement strategies to mitigate negative consequences. Engage with stakeholders and communities to understand and address concerns.

Long-Term Accountability

- Challenge: Ensuring accountability for the long-term impact of digital twins may be challenging, especially as technology evolves.

- Consideration: Establish governance structures, codes of conduct, and accountability mechanisms to ensure responsible use of digital twins. Regularly review and update ethical guidelines as technology and societal norms evolve.

Addressing these ethical considerations requires a proactive and holistic approach that involves collaboration among various stakeholders, including developers, policymakers, ethicists, and the individuals affected by digital twin implementations. By prioritizing ethical considerations, organizations can build trust, promote responsible innovation, and contribute to the positive impact of digital twins on society.

REGULATORY LANDSCAPE

The regulatory landscape for digital twins is evolving as governments and industry bodies recognize the potential impact and challenges associated with this technology. While specific regulations may vary by country and industry, several overarching considerations and frameworks are emerging. Here's an overview of the regulatory landscape for digital twins:

Data Protection and Privacy Regulations

- GDPR (General Data Protection Regulation): In the European Union, GDPR sets guidelines for the processing of personal data. Organizations implementing digital twins must ensure compliance with GDPR, especially when dealing with sensitive or personally identifiable information.

Industry-Specific Regulations

- Healthcare (HIPAA): In the healthcare sector, the Health Insurance Portability and Accountability Act (HIPAA) in the United States sets standards for the protection of patient health information. Digital twins in healthcare must comply with these regulations.

- Finance (PCI DSS): For digital twins used in financial services, compliance with Payment Card Industry Data Security Standard (PCI DSS) is crucial to ensure the security of financial transactions and customer data.

Cybersecurity Regulations

- NIST Cybersecurity Framework: The National Institute of Standards and Technology (NIST) in the United States provides a cybersecurity framework that organizations can use to manage and improve their cybersecurity posture. Adhering to such frameworks is essential for securing digital twin implementations.

Product Liability and Safety Regulations

- ISO 19650 (Building Information Modeling): In construction and infrastructure projects, adherence to standards such as ISO 19650 related to Building Information Modeling (BIM) is essential. It ensures that digital twins in the construction industry meet specific safety and quality standards.

Ethical and Responsible AI Guidelines

- EU AI Act: The European Union is in the process of developing the EU Artificial Intelligence Act, which aims to regulate AI applications. Digital twins incorporating AI may fall under these regulations, especially if they impact critical infrastructure or pose high risks.

Environmental Regulations

- Energy Star Certification: Digital twins in smart buildings and energy management may be subject to environmental regulations and certification programs like Energy Star, which focuses on energy efficiency.

Telecommunications Regulations

- FCC Regulations (in the U.S.): Digital twins involved in telecommunications infrastructure may need to comply with regulations set by the Federal Communications Commission (FCC) in the United States.

Standards and Interoperability

- ISO 23247 (Digital Twin Framework): The International Organization for Standardization (ISO) has developed standards, such as ISO 23247, that provide a framework for digital twins. Compliance with such standards enhances interoperability and consistency across digital twin implementations.

Intellectual Property Laws

- Patents and Copyrights: Organizations developing proprietary algorithms, models, or software components for digital twins may need to consider intellectual property laws to protect their innovations.

Smart City Regulations

- Smart City Guidelines: Some regions have specific guidelines and regulations for the deployment of smart city technologies, which may encompass digital twin applications in urban planning, transportation, and infrastructure management.

Autonomous Systems Regulations

- Regulatory Agencies (e.g., FAA): Digital twins used in conjunction with autonomous systems, such as drones or autonomous vehicles, may need to comply with regulations set by relevant agencies (e.g., Federal Aviation Administration for drones).

Collaborative and Open Data Guidelines

- Open Data Initiatives: In collaborative digital twin environments, adherence to open data initiatives and guidelines can promote transparency and interoperability.

Government Policies and Strategies

- National AI Strategies: Some countries have introduced national AI strategies that may impact the development and deployment of digital twins, especially if AI technologies are integral to their functionality.

Health and Safety Regulations

- OSHA Regulations (Occupational Safety and Health Administration): In industries where digital twins are used for monitoring and optimizing health and safety conditions, compliance with OSHA regulations is critical.

Cross-Border Data Transfer Regulations

- Privacy Shield (for EU-U.S. Data Transfers): For digital twins involving cross-border data transfers, compliance with frameworks like the EU-U.S. Privacy Shield may be necessary to ensure lawful data transfer.

Blockchain and Cryptocurrency Regulations

- Crypto Regulations: In scenarios where blockchain technology is integrated into digital twins, compliance with cryptocurrency and blockchain regulations may be relevant, depending on the application.

Local Regulations and Zoning Laws

- Local Planning Regulations: In the context of digital twins used in urban planning, compliance with local regulations and zoning laws is crucial to ensure alignment with city development plans.

Navigating the regulatory landscape for digital twins requires a comprehensive understanding of the specific industry, geographical location, and the nature of data and processes involved. Organizations should stay informed about emerging regulations, actively engage with relevant authorities, and embed compliance considerations into their digital twin strategies.

COST-BENEFIT ANALYSIS

Conducting a thorough cost-benefit analysis (CBA) is essential before embarking on the implementation of digital twins. A well-structured CBA helps organizations assess the financial viability, risks, and potential returns associated with adopting digital twin technology. Here's a guide on how to perform a cost-benefit analysis for digital twins:

Identify Project Goals and Objectives

- Clearly define the goals and objectives of implementing digital twins. Identify the specific problems or opportunities the digital twin is meant to address, such as improving efficiency, reducing downtime, or enhancing decision-making.

Define Key Performance Indicators (KPIs)

- Establish measurable KPIs that align with the identified goals. These may include improvements in operational efficiency, cost savings, reduced downtime, enhanced predictive maintenance, or improved decision-making speed.

Cost Components

- Development Costs: Include expenses related to software development, data integration, algorithm development, and any hardware or IoT devices required.

- Implementation Costs: Consider costs associated with deploying the digital twin, including training, system integration, and any necessary infrastructure upgrades.

- Operational Costs: Account for ongoing operational expenses, including maintenance, monitoring, and personnel training.

- Data Management Costs: Factor in costs related to data storage, processing, and security measures.

- Hardware and Software Licenses: Include costs associated with acquiring licenses for software and any specialized hardware.

Benefits Components

- Operational Efficiency: Quantify potential gains in operational efficiency, such as reduced downtime, optimized processes, and improved resource utilization.

- Predictive Maintenance: Estimate the cost savings associated with predictive maintenance, including reduced equipment failures and unplanned downtime.

- Improved Decision-Making: Assess the value of enhanced decision-making capabilities, such as faster response times and more informed strategic planning.

- Cost Avoidance: Consider potential cost avoidance, such as preventing equipment breakdowns or mitigating risks before they escalate.

- Revenue Generation: Identify opportunities for revenue generation, such as offering new services or improving product quality.

Timeframe for Analysis

- Define the timeframe over which the cost-benefit analysis will be conducted. Consider short-term and long-term impacts, as the benefits of digital twins may accrue over time.

Quantify Costs

- Assign monetary values to each cost component identified. This includes both one-time and recurring costs. Consider both direct and indirect costs.

Quantify Benefits

- Assign monetary values to each benefit component identified. Use a combination of historical data, industry benchmarks, and expert opinions to estimate the monetary impact of benefits.

Risk Assessment

- Identify potential risks that could impact the implementation of digital twins. Assess the likelihood and potential impact of these risks on both costs and benefits.

Net Present Value (NPV)

- Calculate the Net Present Value to account for the time value of money. This involves discounting future costs and benefits to their present values.

Return on Investment (ROI)

- Calculate the Return on Investment by dividing the net benefits by the total costs and expressing the result as a percentage.

Sensitivity Analysis

- Conduct sensitivity analysis to assess how changes in key assumptions, such as adoption rates, costs, or benefits, may impact the overall outcome of the analysis.

Qualitative Factors

- Consider qualitative factors that may not be easily quantifiable, such as improved customer satisfaction, enhanced brand reputation, or strategic alignment with industry trends.

Compare Scenarios

- Assess different scenarios, such as a phased implementation versus a full-scale deployment, to understand the impact on costs and benefits.

Decision Criteria

- Establish decision criteria based on the results of the analysis. Determine thresholds for ROI or other key metrics that would indicate a successful or unsuccessful outcome.

Continuous Monitoring

- Plan for continuous monitoring and evaluation after the implementation. Regularly assess actual performance against projected benefits and costs to make informed adjustments.

Stakeholder Involvement

- Involve key stakeholders in the cost-benefit analysis process. Gather input from relevant departments, including IT, operations, finance, and executive leadership.

Documentation

- Document the assumptions, methodologies, and data sources used in the cost-benefit analysis. This documentation is essential for transparency and future reference.

A comprehensive cost-benefit analysis provides decision-makers with valuable insights into the financial implications and potential outcomes of digital twin implementation. It serves as a critical tool for informed decision-making, risk management, and ongoing optimization of digital twin strategies.

EDUCATIONAL AND TRAINING IMPLICATIONS

The adoption of digital twins across industries brings about significant implications for education and training. As this technology becomes more prevalent, there is a growing need for individuals with the skills and knowledge to design, implement, and utilize digital twins effectively. Here are key educational and training implications associated with digital twins:

Curriculum Development

- Integration of Digital Twin Concepts: Educational institutions, especially those offering engineering, computer science, and relevant programs, should integrate digital twin concepts into their curricula. This includes understanding the underlying technologies, data science, and domain-specific applications.

Specialized Training Programs

- Professional Development Courses: Offer specialized training programs or short courses for professionals seeking to upskill or reskill in digital twin technologies.

These courses can cover topics such as data modeling, simulation, and real-time data integration.

Collaboration with Industry

- Partnerships with Companies: Educational institutions can establish partnerships with industry players implementing digital twins. This collaboration can provide students with real-world insights, access to industry experts, and opportunities for hands-on experience.

Laboratories and Practical Training

- Digital Twin Laboratories: Establish dedicated laboratories equipped with the necessary hardware and software for students to gain hands-on experience in developing and working with digital twins. Practical training is crucial for skill development.

Interdisciplinary Programs

- Collaboration Across Disciplines: Given the interdisciplinary nature of digital twins, educational institutions should encourage collaboration between students from various disciplines, such as engineering, data science, and business.

Simulation and Virtual Reality Training

- Use of Simulation Tools: Incorporate simulation tools and virtual reality environments into training programs. This allows students to simulate real-world scenarios and interact with digital twins in a controlled and immersive setting.

Case Studies and Projects

- Real-World Projects: Integrate real-world case studies and projects into the curriculum. This exposes students to practical challenges and helps them develop problem-solving skills specific to digital twin applications.

Continuous Learning Platforms

- Online Learning Platforms: Offer online courses and platforms for continuous learning in digital twin technologies. This accommodates professionals looking to update their skills without interrupting their careers.

Certifications in Digital Twin Technologies

- Professional Certifications: Develop certifications that validate individuals' proficiency in digital twin technologies. These certifications can serve as a valuable credential for job seekers and professionals.

Faculty Development

- Training for Educators: Provide training and development opportunities for educators to stay current with advancements in digital twin technologies. This ensures that educators can effectively teach and mentor students.

Soft Skills Development

- Communication and Collaboration Skills: Emphasize the development of soft skills, such as communication and collaboration, as working with digital twins often involves interdisciplinary teamwork and interaction with stakeholders.

Research Opportunities

- Encourage Research Projects: Foster a culture of research and innovation in digital twin technologies. Encourage students and faculty to engage in research projects that contribute to the advancement of the field.

Global Collaboration

- International Collaboration: Facilitate global collaboration and exchange programs with institutions that are leaders in digital twin research and implementation. This exposure enhances students' perspectives and widens their network.

Continuous Industry Engagement

- Industry Advisory Boards: Establish industry advisory boards that provide guidance on the relevance of educational programs to industry needs. Regular input from industry experts ensures alignment with the latest trends and requirements.

Accessibility and Diversity

- Inclusive Education: Ensure that educational programs are accessible and inclusive, considering diverse backgrounds and experiences. This promotes a diverse workforce in the field of digital twins.

Cybersecurity and Ethical Considerations

- Integration of Cybersecurity and Ethics: Include modules on cybersecurity and ethical considerations in digital twin education. As digital twins involve sensitive data and decision-making, students need an understanding of security and ethical best practices.

Adaptability to Technological Advances

- Flexible Curriculum Design: Design curricula that can adapt to rapid technological changes. Digital twin technologies evolve, and educational programs should stay flexible to incorporate emerging trends.

Life-Long Learning Culture

- Promote Continuous Learning: Foster a culture of lifelong learning, encouraging professionals to continuously update their skills to keep pace with advancements in digital twin technologies.

Educational institutions and training providers play a crucial role in preparing the workforce for the era of digital twins. By incorporating these educational and training implications, institutions can equip individuals with the skills and knowledge needed to leverage the full potential of digital twins in various industries.

GLOBAL ADOPTION AND REGIONAL VARIANCES

The adoption of digital twins is a global phenomenon, with organizations worldwide recognizing the transformative potential of this technology. However, the pace and extent of adoption can vary across regions due to factors such as technological readiness, industry focus, regulatory environments, and cultural differences. Here's an overview of global adoption trends and regional variances related to digital twins:

North America

- Adoption Leaders: North America, particularly the United States, is a leader in digital twin adoption. Industries such as manufacturing, healthcare, and infrastructure have embraced digital twins to optimize operations and enhance decision-making.

- Focus on Industry 4.0: The manufacturing sector in the U.S. has been at the forefront, leveraging digital twins within the context of Industry 4.0 initiatives for smart factories.

Europe

- Strong Embrace of Industry 4.0: European countries, especially Germany, have embraced digital twins as part of their Industry 4.0 strategies. Manufacturing, automotive, and aerospace industries have integrated digital twins to improve efficiency and competitiveness.

- EU Regulations and Standards: The European Union's focus on data protection and standardization has influenced how digital twins are implemented, with a strong emphasis on compliance with GDPR and relevant standards.

Asia-Pacific

- Rapid Adoption in Manufacturing: Countries like China and Japan have witnessed rapid adoption of digital twins, particularly in manufacturing. Chinese industries are integrating digital twins to enhance production efficiency and product quality.

- Smart Cities Initiatives: Several Asia-Pacific countries, including Singapore and South Korea, are incorporating digital twins into smart city initiatives for urban planning, infrastructure management, and public services.

Middle East and Africa

- Infrastructure Development: The Middle East, especially in the Gulf Cooperation Council (GCC) countries, is adopting digital twins for large-scale infrastructure projects. Digital twins play a role in construction, urban planning, and facility management.

- Focus on Oil and Gas: Oil-rich countries in the region, such as Saudi Arabia and the United Arab Emirates, are leveraging digital twins in the oil and gas sector for asset management and optimization.

Latin America

- Emerging Adoption: Latin America is in the early stages of adopting digital twins, with increasing interest in sectors like manufacturing, agriculture, and infrastructure.

- Agricultural Applications: In countries like Brazil, digital twins are being explored for precision agriculture to optimize crop management and resource utilization.

Industry-Specific Variances

- Manufacturing Dominance: Manufacturing has been a common focus for digital twin adoption globally, with industries such as automotive, aerospace, and electronics leading the way.

- Healthcare Innovation: Healthcare is a rapidly growing sector for digital twins, with applications ranging from personalized medicine to hospital operations optimization. Adoption patterns vary based on the healthcare system structure in different regions.

Regulatory Variances

- GDPR Influence in Europe: European countries are particularly sensitive to data protection, influenced by GDPR. This has implications for how digital twins handle and protect sensitive information.

- Regulatory Approaches in Asia: In Asia, regulatory approaches may vary, with some countries adopting a more flexible stance to encourage innovation, while others prioritize data security and privacy.

Cultural and Organizational Differences

- Risk Aversion: Cultural factors influence risk tolerance, impacting the speed of adoption. Some regions may be more risk-averse, while others may embrace innovation more readily.

- Organizational Readiness: The readiness of organizations to adopt new technologies can vary. Industries with a strong innovation culture and digital maturity tend to adopt digital twins more quickly.

Connectivity and Infrastructure

- Digital Infrastructure: Regions with advanced digital infrastructure, including high-speed internet and widespread IoT connectivity, are more conducive to seamless digital twin implementations.
- Challenges in Developing Regions: Developing regions may face challenges related to connectivity and infrastructure, potentially slowing down the adoption of digital twins.

Global Technology Providers

- Global Tech Companies' Impact: Global technology providers, irrespective of their origin, play a significant role in shaping digital twin adoption worldwide. Companies like Microsoft, Siemens, and IBM are key players driving global standards and best practices.

Impact of COVID-19

- Acceleration of Digital Transformation: The COVID-19 pandemic has accelerated digital transformation initiatives globally, including the adoption of digital twins. Organizations are increasingly recognizing the need for resilient and data-driven operations.

Future Trends and Convergence

- Convergence of Technologies: The future may witness a convergence of digital twins with other emerging technologies like edge computing, blockchain, and artificial intelligence, influencing global adoption trends.

As digital twin technologies continue to evolve, regional disparities in adoption are likely to narrow, especially as industries recognize the potential for improved efficiency, cost savings, and innovation. Global collaboration, standardization efforts, and knowledge exchange will play crucial roles in shaping a more consistent and widespread adoption of digital twins across diverse regions.

ENVIRONMENTAL SUSTAINABILITY

The implementation of digital twins has the potential to contribute to environmental sustainability by fostering efficiency, reducing resource consumption, and enabling proactive environmental management. Here are key considerations and ways in which digital twins can support environmental sustainability:

Energy Efficiency

- Optimized Operations: Digital twins facilitate the optimization of operations in various industries, leading to reduced energy consumption. For example, in smart buildings, digital twins can optimize HVAC systems, lighting, and energy usage based on real-time data.

Resource Management

- Smart Agriculture: In agriculture, digital twins help optimize irrigation, crop monitoring, and fertilization, leading to more efficient resource utilization and reduced environmental impact.

- Water and Waste Management: Digital twins can be applied in urban planning and infrastructure to monitor and manage water distribution, wastewater treatment, and waste disposal, minimizing environmental harm.

Predictive Maintenance

- Reduced E-Waste: In manufacturing and industrial settings, digital twins enable predictive maintenance, ensuring that equipment is serviced before failure. This minimizes unplanned downtime and reduces the need for premature replacement, thereby decreasing electronic waste.

Transportation and Logistics

- Smart Logistics: Digital twins in transportation and logistics optimize routes, reduce fuel consumption, and enhance supply chain efficiency, contributing to lower carbon emissions.

- Electric Vehicle Integration: In the automotive sector, digital twins can support the design and optimization of electric vehicles, contributing to the transition to cleaner transportation options.

Urban Planning and Design

- Smart Cities: Digital twins play a crucial role in smart city initiatives by providing insights into urban infrastructure, traffic flow, and energy usage. This can lead to more sustainable urban planning and development.

- Green Building Design: In construction, digital twins support the design and construction of green buildings, considering factors such as energy efficiency, sustainable materials, and waste reduction.

Remote Monitoring and Control

- Reduced Travel: Digital twins enable remote monitoring and control of various systems, reducing the need for physical presence. This can result in decreased travel-related carbon emissions.

Simulation for Sustainable Solutions

- Environmental Impact Assessment: Digital twins allow for the simulation and assessment of environmental impacts before the physical implementation of projects. This is particularly relevant in industries such as construction and infrastructure development.

Precision Agriculture

- Reduced Chemical Usage: In agriculture, digital twins support precision farming practices, optimizing the use of pesticides and fertilizers. This precision can reduce chemical runoff and its impact on ecosystems.

Circular Economy Practices

- Lifecycle Management: Digital twins support the monitoring and management of product lifecycles. This can contribute to the adoption of circular economy practices by promoting recycling, reusing, and refurbishing products.

Data-Driven Environmental Monitoring

- Real-time Environmental Monitoring: Digital twins can integrate real-time data from sensors and IoT devices to monitor environmental conditions. This capability is valuable for tracking air quality, pollution levels, and biodiversity.

Collaborative Ecosystems

- Shared Resources: In collaborative digital twin ecosystems, different stakeholders can share resources and information, promoting more efficient use of materials and reducing duplication of efforts.

Green Data Centers

- Energy-Efficient Computing: Organizations implementing digital twins can prioritize the use of green data centers and energy-efficient computing practices to minimize the environmental impact of data processing.

Supply Chain Transparency

- Sustainable Sourcing: Digital twins enable supply chain transparency, allowing organizations to track and verify the sustainability of raw materials and components throughout the supply chain.

Renewable Energy Integration

- Smart Grids: In the energy sector, digital twins contribute to the development of smart grids, optimizing the integration of renewable energy sources and enhancing overall grid efficiency.

Environmental Compliance

- Regulatory Adherence: Digital twins assist industries in monitoring and ensuring compliance with environmental regulations, reducing the likelihood of environmental violations.

Continuous Improvement

- Feedback Loops: Through continuous monitoring and analysis, digital twins provide feedback loops that can be used to identify opportunities for further environmental improvements and sustainability initiatives.

Eco-Friendly Product Design

- Life Cycle Assessment: Digital twins support life cycle assessments of products, aiding in the design of eco-friendly products with minimal environmental impact.

- While digital twins offer significant potential for environmental sustainability, it's crucial to approach their implementation responsibly. This includes considering the environmental impact of the technologies themselves, ensuring data security to prevent environmental harm, and continuously assessing and improving sustainability practices associated with digital twin implementations.

CONTINUOUS IMPROVEMENT AND ITERATIVE DEVELOPMENT

Continuous improvement and iterative development are fundamental principles for the successful implementation and evolution of digital twins. These approaches enable organizations to adapt to changing requirements, incorporate user feedback, and enhance the overall effectiveness of digital twin solutions. Here's a breakdown of the key concepts and strategies associated with continuous improvement and iterative development in the context of digital twins:

Continuous Improvement

1. Feedback Loops:

- Establish mechanisms for collecting feedback from users, stakeholders, and real-world performance data. Continuous improvement relies on a feedback loop that informs adjustments and enhancements to the digital twin.

2. Data Analytics and Insights:

- Leverage data analytics tools to extract meaningful insights from the performance data of the digital twin.

Analyze trends, identify areas for improvement, and use data-driven decision-making to guide enhancements.

3. Key Performance Indicators (KPIs):

- Define and regularly review KPIs that align with the overarching goals of the digital twin. Monitoring key metrics allows organizations to assess performance and identify opportunities for refinement.

4. Benchmarking and Best Practices:

- Stay informed about industry benchmarks and best practices. Regularly compare the performance of the digital twin against established standards, and implement improvements to align with or exceed industry norms.

5. Cross-Functional Collaboration:

- Foster collaboration between different departments and teams involved in the digital twin ecosystem. Cross-functional input can provide diverse perspectives and contribute to holistic improvements.

6. Agile Principles:

- Apply agile development principles, such as sprint planning, regular retrospectives, and adaptive planning.

Agile methodologies facilitate continuous improvement by allowing teams to respond quickly to changing requirements.

7. User-Centric Design:

- Prioritize user experience and usability. Gather feedback directly from end-users to understand their needs and preferences, and incorporate this feedback into the design and functionality of the digital twin.

8. Strategic Roadmaps:

- Develop strategic roadmaps that outline the evolution of the digital twin over time. This roadmap should incorporate planned improvements, new features, and iterative releases to address identified shortcomings.

9. Lean Principles:

- Embrace lean principles to eliminate waste and optimize processes. Regularly assess the efficiency of digital twin workflows and make adjustments to streamline operations.

Iterative Development

1. Minimum Viable Product (MVP):

- Start with a minimum viable product that addresses the core functionalities and objectives of the digital twin. Iterate on this foundation based on user feedback and evolving requirements.

2. Prototyping and Testing:

- Use prototyping and testing to experiment with new features or enhancements. This iterative approach allows organizations to validate concepts before committing to full-scale development.

3. Incremental Releases:

- Release updates and improvements incrementally rather than waiting for a complete overhaul. This approach ensures that users benefit from enhancements more frequently and reduces the risk of major disruptions.

4. Adaptive Design:

- Design the digital twin architecture to be adaptive and modular. This enables the integration of new functionalities and components without major disruptions to existing systems.

5. Version Control:

- Implement version control mechanisms to track changes and updates to the digital twin. This ensures that organizations can roll back changes if issues arise and maintain a clear record of the system's evolution.

6. Cross-Platform Compatibility:

- Ensure cross-platform compatibility to support the integration of new technologies and devices. An iterative approach allows organizations to adapt to emerging platforms and technologies seamlessly.

7. Scalability Planning:

- Consider scalability from the outset and plan for iterative enhancements to accommodate growing data volumes, user bases, and evolving business requirements.

8. Continuous Testing:

- Implement continuous testing practices to identify and address issues early in the development cycle. Automated testing tools can streamline the testing process, ensuring reliability with each iteration.

9. Collaborative Development Teams:

- Foster collaboration among development teams, operations, and other stakeholders. Cross-functional collaboration enhances communication, accelerates development cycles, and supports the iterative release of new features.

10. Risk Mitigation:

- Identify potential risks early in the development process. Iterative development allows for the incorporation of risk mitigation strategies and adjustments based on real-world performance and feedback.

11. Scrum and DevOps Practices:

- Adopt Scrum methodologies and DevOps practices to facilitate iterative development, continuous integration, and continuous delivery. These methodologies enhance collaboration and support a culture of continuous improvement.

12. Documentation and Knowledge Sharing:

- Maintain comprehensive documentation to capture the evolution of the digital twin. Knowledge sharing ensures that insights gained from previous iterations are preserved and can inform future developments.

By combining continuous improvement and iterative development strategies, organizations can build resilient, adaptive, and effective digital twins. These approaches foster a culture of innovation, responsiveness to user needs, and the ongoing evolution of digital twin solutions in alignment with organizational goals and industry advancements.

CONCLUSION AND IMPACT

In conclusion, digital twins have emerged as transformative tools with profound implications across various industries. The journey from concept to implementation has seen the convergence of technologies such as IoT, AI, and data analytics, giving rise to dynamic virtual representations that mirror the physical world. The impact of digital twins extends far beyond individual sectors, influencing how businesses operate, innovate, and make data-driven decisions. Here's a summary of the conclusion and the broad impact of digital twins:

KEY TAKEAWAYS:

Holistic Understanding:

- Digital twins provide a holistic understanding of physical assets, processes, and systems, enabling organizations to gain actionable insights and optimize performance.

Real-time Monitoring and Control

- The real-time monitoring and control capabilities of digital twins empower organizations to respond swiftly to changes, predict issues before they occur, and enhance overall operational efficiency.

Interdisciplinary Collaboration:

- Digital twins foster interdisciplinary collaboration, breaking down silos and promoting a holistic approach to problem-solving. Teams from engineering, IT, data science, and other domains collaborate to achieve common objectives.

Predictive Maintenance and Optimization:

- Predictive maintenance, enabled by digital twins, minimizes downtime, extends the lifespan of assets, and optimizes resource utilization. Industries can move from reactive to proactive maintenance strategies.

Data-driven Decision-Making:

- Digital twins leverage vast amounts of data to facilitate data-driven decision-making. This shift enhances the accuracy of decision-making processes, reducing uncertainty and improving overall business outcomes.

Innovation and Product Development:

- The application of digital twins in innovation and product development accelerates the design and testing phases, reducing time-to-market and enabling organizations to bring innovative products and solutions to consumers faster.

Enhanced Customer Experience:

- Digital twins contribute to enhanced customer experiences by enabling personalized services, improving product quality, and providing better support and maintenance services.

Sustainability and Environmental Impact:

- Digital twins play a role in sustainability efforts by optimizing resource consumption, supporting precision agriculture, reducing energy usage, and contributing to overall environmental stewardship.

Continuous Improvement Culture:

- The adoption of digital twins encourages a culture of continuous improvement and iterative development. Organizations evolve their digital twins over time, responding to feedback, adapting to changing requirements, and staying at the forefront of technological advancements.

OVERALL IMPACT

Operational Efficiency:

- Digital twins fundamentally enhance operational efficiency by providing real-time visibility, predictive capabilities, and data-driven insights, leading to streamlined processes and reduced operational costs.

Competitive Advantage:

- Organizations leveraging digital twins gain a competitive advantage by staying agile, responsive to market changes, and capable of delivering innovative solutions faster than their competitors.

Risk Mitigation:

- Predictive analytics and simulation capabilities in digital twins contribute to effective risk mitigation strategies. Organizations can identify and address potential issues before they escalate, minimizing risks associated with operational disruptions.

Cost Savings:

- Through optimized operations, predictive maintenance, and efficient resource utilization, digital twins contribute to significant cost savings over the life cycle of assets and processes.

Transformation Across Industries:

- Digital twins have a broad impact across diverse industries, including manufacturing, healthcare, construction, energy, smart cities, and more. Their adaptability makes them a transformative force in addressing industry-specific challenges.

Innovation Ecosystems:

- Digital twins contribute to the development of innovation ecosystems, where organizations collaborate, share data, and collectively drive advancements in technology and industry practices.

Human-Machine Collaboration:

- The human-machine collaboration facilitated by digital twins augments human capabilities, fostering a symbiotic relationship between humans and intelligent systems. This collaboration results in more informed decision-making and optimized processes.

Long-term Value Creation:

- Digital twins create long-term value by supporting the entire life cycle of assets and processes. Their adaptability ensures that organizations can evolve and extract value over extended periods.

In summary, the journey of digital twins from concept to widespread implementation represents a paradigm shift in how organizations leverage technology to understand, optimize, and innovate in the physical world. As technology continues to advance, the impact of digital twins is expected to deepen, influencing not only how businesses operate but also how societies manage resources, respond to challenges, and envision a more connected and intelligent future.